D1605961

ON GHOSTS

ON GHOSTS

Elizabeth Robinson

SOLID OBJECTS

NEW YORK

Printed in Canada

Design by Erik Rieselbach

Grateful acknowledgment is made to the editors of *Sidebrow*, in which a portion
of this work first appeared, and to the Djerassi Resident Artists Program.

Unattributed quotes come from Robin Blaser and Barbara Guest.
—E. R.

ISBN-13: 978-0-9844142-6-0
ISBN-10: 0-9844142-6-6

Library of Congress Control Number: 2013937583

SOLID OBJECTS
P.O. Box 296
New York, NY 10113

For Jeffrey Robinson

ON GHOSTS

"I am the ghost of answering questions. Beware me.
Keep me at a distance as I keep you at a distance."
—Jack Spicer

Explanatory Note

This is an essay on the phenomenon of ghosts and haunting. It arises in relation to the possibility that a self or a site might be haunted. I do not take this phenomenon to be negative or positive, only neutral. As I understand it, this occurrence reveals little about phantoms and visitations and is more disclosive of conditions that locate themselves in specific sites or persons. These conditions calibrate individuals or places, make them vulnerable to the heightened perception, which is hauntedness.

Being haunted, becoming aware of the presence of presence, would in some sense be ordinary then. The perceiver might be a sieve that experience falls through. The perceiver might be a mirror bouncing light from one source into the mundane world of his or her daily life. I posit that both things take place at once.

Example:
I was recently introduced to a building, which I had been told had been infested with termites. Standing outside, I looked at the support beams. They had indeed been consumed by pests: it looked like the roof was being supported by long narrow sponges. The owner of the building had recently repainted the building, and the porous beams threw off a lustrous gleam.

Because I am examining the ways a perceiver encounters an oblique and dubious phenomenon, my discussion will be mediated correspondingly. That is, firstly, no one can fairly circumscribe a base level, a ground of knowledge for spirits and their sites. Secondly, it should be taken for granted that the perceiver is not privileged. Rather, the perceiver is prepared for the experience on the basis of his or her having, so to speak, been eaten by pests. The condition is one of eroded defenses, of vulnerability.

Vulnerability may react with a direct counter-defensiveness, but that is not the mode I anticipate or understand to be in play here. The essay will necessarily operate circuitously. Its manner will be disorganized where it accurately follows the movement of the uncircumscribable through the deteriorated soul, through wormhole, pest warren, glare.

4

To commence:

The apparition is not the entity that haunts. What it is, instead, is more like metaphysical sandpaper. It debrides, taking away all the dead tissue, and some of the living tissue. "Ghost," with its connotation of white mist or film, is misleading. Think witch hazel or another astringent agent. Think of a scent whose sharpness makes you sneeze.

When the apparition has whittled down your resistance, then you are less of who you are than you used to be.

This lessening is the mode of the haunting. There's now a little alleyway, between the self and the not-self, newly arrived, and this alley gives free passage to come-who-will, or what-will. The nouns are difficult and misleading here. What is it that makes free passage? The new not-selfness is exquisitely sensitive to presence but by its own absence has been thrown into the realm of the nonlinguistic.

What is so evidently not there is just as evidently having its way. Presence, then, is a *way*.

The self has a séance with its own-ness, with its leaving off. The body is the table on which all manifest clicks and taps occur.

Finding a way.

The apparition or ghost or spirit wants to find a way *out*.

But as I said, apparition is not an entity as we think of it. Rough erasure, but not real agency, not "power." The ability to take away is not, in this realm, a power. It is palimpsest, implicit disclosure.

Think sweating fieldworkers hacking away, almost randomly, at underbrush. The "trail" they open is still choked with stems and branches and doesn't go clearly to any particular place.

Presence then is a way, but not a particular way. Its opening discloses an opening. Did the ghost get out? This might be an irrelevant question. But that it is a question *is* relevant.

"Ideas come and settle in my mind by mistake, then, realizing their mistake, they absolutely insist on coming out."
—Simone Weil

Creatures

The subject has had trouble shaking the pain caused by injury. Her preoccupation with pain permits the pain to become parasitic. It eats through layers of her self variably, mostly consuming the surface, but sometimes penetrating deeper. The remainder of the surface is first spongy with this excavation, but then dries to a surprising sheen.

Light-reflecting surfaces can also seem to be light-bearing surfaces. They attract things that want light. They are attractive.

The subject begins to complain that she feels invisible "creatures" piggybacking on her. She is not satisfied with the term "creatures" but no other term offers itself for use.

Even "use" returns as astringent, as frictive, as burrowing, as diminishing. The subject develops the desire to live in a world without use. If she is to be flayed of her injury, then she wants to retain the shine of that nakedness and not bear the weight of other, appending, presence.

Where she is not, she wants nothing else.

The Soul

The soul in its doorway

and then the doorway dies.

This is misbehavior.

Each soul is a kind of manna

on itself. A doorway that recedes

in size until perspective tells kind

falsehoods: that the doorway is fitted

to the soul. Slick manna of meaning is soul's

parasitical soul. This is not good.

Goodness does not have structure.

The soul loves a termite's logic of

structure: it eats it. Soul reproduces itself

a hundred, no, a thousand times and eats

itself. Infinitesimal teeth make pearly dust.

The soul compels love and extermination. By taking away
the larger structure, each of us souls acquires many,
many smaller structures. A home inside pearly
dust. The tooth's logic is the doorway.

Manna spoils if not eaten immediately. Around us,
we see it descend. It tells us we are one: be united.
I see it descend. I see the doorway cut into the belly
of the manna. Soul, disclose this soul. Madly repeat
yourself. Like a fine mist in the air, one
doorway thrown open after another. Until the portal
states its purpose: disgorge purpose. We are one
pulse, particulate and tinting the atmosphere.
We see the spoils descend. Immediately:
surround us. All souls. I aspirate. I surround
us.

Faith will brandish the blade that

will cut toward the inner workings. Hence

the inner workings escape, and slip around

to the door, and there they shrink and

make the soul's perfect structural opacity.

Only repetition does violence, but that

is no shirking of the good. The necessary

good. The good constraining of the doorway:

we do as I, immediately, sink down into it. I do believe

the soul's logic is good.

Definitely Documentary

Narrative is a falsification, but still, inside it, strange things begin to happen. The following should be considered as documentary.

The semi-arid plain becomes a forest. There is no justification for this.

A plague sweeps the forest that surmounted or undergirded the newly appeared forest, turning it rust and dead.

But "our" forest is unperturbed. Its wolves and dogs stroll untended in its licorice-green shade.

Alpine Egypt.

Another plague comes and infects the ferrets and the prairie dogs. Sick, they nip at the heels of the pedestrians, the ones who hold leashes, who exchange pleasantries with names at the ends of the leashes.

This no fairy tale, but pure reportage. In the same way, the mountain lion lay down and slept in the domestic shrubs beside the deer he had killed and partially eaten.

*

I'd like to clarify. If the full belly is haunted, then ghosts are a satiation. They satiate themselves. The carcass is the site of the visitation and for that reason it needs must be incomplete. One spirit or another has the responsibility for gnawing on it.

Incident One

A child ends his own life. How, we do not know. We do not even know if he was a boy when his life ended. But it is over.

Over and over the loop of his life rubs on its seam until the stitches rough up his skin and the garment comes apart. Dual ravel.

He wrestles in the hammock slung over *what*, until seam and skin fall out.

How can a child figure this out, what to do with goneness, clearly clumsy. The one who made himself go away has gone away and then what to do? He keeps coming back to his departure.

This is how his movement develops as movement, a return. This how return becomes an irritant:

*the nicely watered grass gets trodden down and the soil beneath it glistens, clinging to the bottoms of shoes

*the seams between shoulder and armpit pull loose

*the sleeper wakes up with a full bladder and falls over in the dark on the way to the toilet. Again. Falls over, barking up the shin again. Goes back to bed again. Again

*the tape clicks on mid-narrative when no one is there to push the PLAY button on

*the child likes TV, watches commercials, hums their refrains incessantly

PHOTOGRAPH #1

This is a photograph of a domestic interior. Because this ghost manifested primarily in an auditory manner, it is hard to see anything of significance in this photo. Note however the ghost's baby tooth crumbling in a dish on the kitchen counter (foreground) and further back in the room, the boom box that went on at random times, always when there was a Harry Potter story tape in it.

The Relation of Mother and Child
to Haunting and Ghost

Another child speculates that it is in the nature of the ghost to be broken.

(See poem below).

What a canny insight for a child to have, in particular a child who sleeps through visitations.

From this the self continues on to wonder: of what unbroken, or whole, model is the ghost a broken version? By now, even the child probably knows that humans are not whole. In what way is a ghost broken, and if it were a crushed teacup, glued painstakingly back together, what would emerge? Most likely it would be only a teacup. A receptacle, or a disguise, but in either case no longer watertight.

When the mother extolled her son, saying what a powerful idea, how insightful for the child to have intuited that ghosts are damaged specimens, broken from what they had originally been (though she said it more directly and with less opaque language) the son looked at her blankly. As though he had no idea what conversation she was referencing.

Blank memory is not the same as broken memory. The ghost is broken, but the memory has been taken completely away. That is the efficacy of the broken thing, to enact a removal, to study absence and to ape it.

In the game

who was it   Someone

      said to pick the ghost

Why

or

Y

      and the very token of it

          was mist in the hand

Why the hand

and   whose?

                Someone

We did recall

That the road branched

      like a "Y"

      You pick the ghost because

"all ghosts are broken"

a game or a divining rod

as though   *someone*   could, after all,

        choose

    when the choice was overhead, soft and balmy and broken

        where the hand branched, why, to trace the vapor

Getaway

Several instances redound to narrative arc.

The self with its piggyback counterweight.

The means of escape that the self provides but cannot, itself, put to use.

The injustice that heightens perception supernaturally.

The claim that capitalizes on itself.

Where absence is desire that does not result from, or indicate, lack, but creates avenue.

Every road unpaved, poorly marked, unsafe, a hazarded guess. The French took down road signs, after all, to confuse Germans during the Occupation.

Analogy:

You can arrange the page and enumerate all the propositions you like, but this is a page, and words may irritate its surface, dog-ear and crease it, but they will never truly impact the surface, and they will never escape their page.

Perhaps this is a spurious analogy.

Elsewhere we studied the writer, and we asked, What was his body, what was his soul, what was the word to him? We concluded that the word, his word or words, was like an autoimmune disease which attacked him, the word's own organism, his soul and his body. This may be the better analogy.

Incident Two

I felt suddenly sorry that I hadn't been in contact with my grandmother, for whom I was named. She was then very old and physically fragile, and, lately, not very well oriented. I wrote her a letter. I told her about San Francisco, and gave some mundane details of my life there. I had just gone to New York, so I recounted wandering past a flea market on Houston St. where I found and bought an antique silver necklace, cast of acorns. It prickled my neck when I wore it.

About three days later, my father called me to tell me that my grandmother had died. He loved his mother, but when I asked him if he was okay, he replied brusquely, "I'm all right." He asked me to write a eulogy for her. A few days later I flew down to Los Angeles for her funeral.

There were very few of us present. It was an awkward affair at Forest Lawn, presided over by a young minister, a woman, who was kind but seemed embarrassed by her youth and inexperience. I was wearing a necklace my grandmother had given me and which had also belonged to her mother, all three of us having been named _____. Because I cry easily, my cousin agreed to read my eulogy in which I reminded everyone there of my grandmother's extreme shyness, but also her Britishness, her love of music and reading, and her excellent cookery: "You don't like it. Why are you having some more?"

It was impossible to discuss her without also mentioning her tentativeness, her horror of discomfiting anyone else.

This was so marked a trait in her that it could ironically cause others discomfort while she, say, second-guessed the family, trying to figure out which seat in the car would be the least obtrusive place for her to sit, or what to order at a restaurant: Should she order what someone else was having because that would indicate such a choice was appropriate, or should she order the cheapest entrée?

After the service, everyone drove back to my parents' house where we had an early dinner and told stories about my grandmother and, in some cases, her mother, how they had sailed in steerage from Blackpool and come to Ellis Island.

As the day wound down, my aunt, whom I had not seen in several years, asked me how I liked living in San Francisco. Very much, I told her. Yes, she said, walking through Golden Gate Park each day must be a pleasure. It is, I said with some surprise. She asked me a few more questions, in the course of which I began to feel confused by her astuteness—unsure how she knew so well my current likes and dislikes. Then she said, Too bad you are not wearing your acorn necklace. Well, I replied, automatically, it irritates my neck if I wear it too long. But then I looked at her startled: How did you know about that? My aunt laughed. Your letter for Grandma arrived the day after she died, so we opened it and read it.

Aftermath

Now, was it right for them to have opened the letter and read it? Is mail addressed to an absent recipient legitimately opened by anyone who finds it?

After her funeral, my uncle had told us that he had read Beatrix Potter stories to my grandmother during the last week of her life, and that she had liked this, though, at the same time, she had been preoccupied with inconveniencing him, of being, herself, "a flop."

I think of my grandmother fearing that she was dying clumsily, incorrectly. If this is sad, it is also continuous with her concerns throughout life.

That to be alive is in so many ways to be haunted anyway, to be coursed through with hesitations.

Faltering

My grandmother would not know what to do when she died,
where exactly to go, how to claim her modest packet of life.

She would not know if it was appropriate to send immaterial,
posthumous messages of good-bye.

What my aunt did, what I perceived as a mild invasion of pri-
vacy and a slightly mean joke—confusing me by feeding back
information from the letter I'd sent to my grandmother
        —in this I see the trace of my grandmother.

In the literal sense, I see reflected back my shared conversation
with her, our interest in travel and whimsies. But I also see her
vacillation, her wavering at the doorway: which way?

The vaguest of ghosts, the most oblique. Registering my mes-
sage to her, she sent one back to me, yet she was concerned
with the possible impropriety of her ghosthood.

And so it arrived, but with such timidity that it was almost un-
readable, almost obscured in the guise of practical joke.

PHOTOGRAPH #2

This photograph simply shows the two necklaces mentioned in the anecdote, the one my grandmother gave me, and the one that I told her about in my letter. The letter which my aunt and uncle opened following my grandmother's death has long been destroyed as of the time of this writing.

Skepticism

Any reasonable person will see the implausibility of the story I just related. Any person might reasonably read the letter of a just-deceased person. It might be comforting to do so.

My grandmother did not ghost me.

It's not the question of ghosting that arises here, it's the question of doubt.

Magic, it might be, is the doubting of doubt. It might be. While the doubting of doubt might be at the heart of bereavement, the ugly gap where the ghost gets in, gets in with his or her serum of doubt, which doubtless overflows its leaky cup.

(Late in life, my grandmother always had a handkerchief in hand because her eyes were apt to tear up. She found this humiliating and insisted that it didn't have to do with any excess of emotion. In the past couple of years, I've become subject to the same condition. My optometrist explained that the problem, paradoxically, is that my eyes are so very dry. The tears gush up to compensate for what isn't there.)

What the Ghost Said to Me

Or a series of ghosts. But never with such frankness: The hesitance of ghosts works out as vindictiveness.

As with life, "life"—so much of our agency is inadvertent.

> After he died, he very surely came back to me in my
> dream, but whenever anyone else entered the room of
> the dream, he feigned sleep. This made me look like a
> fool, but I was willing and so I willed it.

Otherwise, I woke up and ran as fast as I could to the room furthest from the room of the dream where I would lean against the wall clutching the muscles of my stomach so that I could keep them inside me, so that they wouldn't get out and contaminate the self that called itself my outside.

"It's always the broken that holds the universe in place.

That's what I would say about poetry and prayer.

That God or audience—the intended direction of both of
those—we wish and wish are real."
—Kazim Ali

Formulae

This is the equation:

too much time/time eternal

_____

too much time in too small a space

Ground down in a pestle as formula:

time quickly dissipating

_____

desperation overlapping with insight

Stated otherwise:
"I've written only one song says the ghostly songwriter,
but I gave it away in a whistle."

—B. J. Love

Translation

On the unsteady ground laid above, I am drop-
ping loss upon loss each time I try this.
Everything you see on the page is a ghost of
something no more corporeal than my breathing
in and out! Then the translations are ghosts
of ghosts, and the voice I give them is at best
a mockery of their past life. I fear I cannot
walk this terrain without falling into chasms
of self: self-interest, self-pity. How will I
be sure that the spirit is speaking in me at
all, much less when I transcribe, much much
less when I translate?

—James Longley

Self and voice fell down the well,
excavating its watery shell.
Doggerel Ghost then hauled them up
and offered them a broken cup.

Doggerel Ghost can speak in tongues.
From the wetness of spirit he twists and is wrung.
Thirsty language wants to sip from this vessel
but the language of Ghost never sates, only wrestles.

Splash: and the Ghost sings from a code:
irritant, error, self-song, and ode.
So the student of tongues becomes a ghost
and the betrayer of saying his impeccable host.

He says,
"The God with whom I was partnered in my time learning to speak in tongues is no longer in/with/above me. Even when He was, the question of who was speaking was difficult."

Visitor

The dead man could not remember me. In our encounter, he repeatedly asked his companion who I was, how I had arrived, what my role was. I claimed to be a teacher, and there I was with him, before my students. This seemed, apparently, implausible to him. Yet he was charming as he read his poems, insisting that he'd never read them to others before. Maybe that was true. He asked again who I was, and I was embarrassed in front of my students because it was I who had invited him to come. "Why, I've never read these poems to anyone before. I'm enjoying it so much! I just want to go on."

The dead man could not remember me. He repeatedly asked his companion who I was, what was my role there. His companion in effect translated this concern again and again, but gracefully. My students were silent, and I felt my sitting there, also silent, made me too prominent, like a bare light bulb. But the dead man read his poems with vigor and elegance, insisting that he'd never read them to others before. Maybe that was true.

Later, or maybe just elsewhere, he said, "where he found the ghosts and so settled on the word and a newly posed language ... [so] it is, I assume,

with one writer after another

that the loosened, embattled relation to meaning, as that

condition informs any meaningful life,

turns up the ghosts—"

PHOTOGRAPH #3

The account from the previous page does not describe an incident in the same way that my other reports do, since the subject was not yet entirely dead, and therefore his status as a ghost is debatable. All the same, I provide the following picture. The ghost is seen looking jaunty, surrounded by a group of friends and admirers. He holds a cigarette aloft.

Dear Ones,

B_____'s mother, I_____, has passed away following open heart surgery. I received this message from B_____ regarding an experience she had soon after her mother's passing:

Before she went in for her operation she and I obviously talked about the possibility of her dying. She said she would send me two grey doves to let me know she was alright.

I must say I thought "oh yes? We have those big grey doves that belong to a house over the way and fly around quite a lot, so how will I know the ones are the ones you sent?"

This morning, as I was on the way to talk to the funeral director, just before I got into my truck, I heard an odd sound and looked up....

There, in the tall spindly tree near our mailbox were 2 grey doves—way smaller than any I have seen in this area before.

So, she kept her word ;-)

I wanted to share this with you all,
J.

Nursery Rhyme

The ghost by nature is a confusion. In the ghost, we are forced to play even if play is not the mode we want to adopt.

Ring-around-a-rosy.

The ghost begins with a circle, with the circular. Imagine that we are all forced to hold hands. Imagine that we are all forced to serve as circumference.

A ghost is by definition broken. A ghost is at the center. The pattern here is not verifiable. We are forced not only to witness the unverifiable, but also to face into it.

Our backs, as we circle around, lie in unprotected darkness. Our faces, our bellies, our breasts, we now know, are part of the broken interior. We are forced to mark the boundary by breaking through its skin with our skin.

A warren of circles.

Incident Three

He was a vindictive man and his ghost was consistent with that.

Have I mentioned him before? He haunted most persistently before he died.

Packages at the door, phone calls, emails, public denunciations. DO NOT

under any circumstances return to me what I have sent to you. This is what he said. Could there be any more eloquent statement marking the behavior of the ghost?

I did not dare to hope that he would die. He enlisted all the populations in his power in an effort to force me to reply to his—what is the word for this?—not just abuse but his *incessantness*. There is another mark of the ghost. Absent or present, always incessant.

The days just prior to his death, though I didn't know he was dying, I felt a sense of release. They were the very last days of the year. I'd had a month or more without any harassment from him. I went to bed shortly after midnight, the turn of the year. My older son had gone to sleep complaining of a stomachache, so I slept, maybe lightly, with that awareness.

About 4:30 or 5:00 A.M., I felt a sharp rap on my shoulder, on the bone. It would be slightly bruised for the next two days. I sat up abruptly, since my son has been known to vomit on sleeping parents. No one was there. There was no one there. Jarred, I lay down again and pulled the covers up to my face. I closed my eyes. A hand roughly grabbed the blanket and pulled it down. I sat up and waited it out.

I had the sensation of an angry person scowling at me. I thought it was another ghost, that of the boy, but I couldn't understand why he had returned, and why he would now be angry. In the blank darkness, I felt there was a suggestion of a shape, but mostly a sensation of irate expectation. It was very definitely a standoff.

After a while, I asked myself if I felt I was in any danger, and I decided not. I did not feel welcome, and this in my own house, but I suddenly felt exhausted as well. Staring at the spot of energy, I lay down again, and waited, and eventually I fell asleep and when I woke up the day was in motion. January 1.

When my friend called to tell me that the old man had died, my first worry was that now that a body did not hamper him he could come back and stalk me with even greater facility, with even more invasiveness. He had even written his obituary himself, in the first person present tense, as though to pervade all our futures with his present, but he did not come back to bother me again.

PHOTOGRAPH #4

Because the bedroom is dim, it is hard to make out any figure.
Look to the upper right of the frame for a gray smudge. It looks
a little bit like a scowling face.

What is "Alive"?

Nearby, the prairie dogs dig so ardently in the soil (here I accidentally wrote "soul" for "soil") that the ground becomes treacherous. Watch out that it doesn't cave in beneath you, that you don't twist your ankle.

The greater danger is from plague that resurges here almost every year.

They look benign, don't they? Small, sociable, pervasive.

They will colonize anywhere, somehow thwarting barriers, eating all the vegetation until the surface of the ground looks scorched.

So the witness, the one who walks over and through, is not a ghost, but shoulders the burdens of the ghost. She can't tell soil from soul. She walks agitatedly over the ground in estimation of where the solid is vacant, where it is crabbed with habitation, the danger of the unoccupied and its susceptibility to being taken over.

Drifting Interlude

"The poem is the unburdening of ghosts of the past who have
come to haunt the writer exposed to the labyrinth."

She comes in from out of doors and asks, abstractedly,

"Is there weather in here?"

"These are ghosts not words;"

Or otherwise, she looks down

and clutches her thigh. Distressed:

"But is this *real*?"

"They are the ephemera that surround and decorate the mind
of the poet."

She says, gesturing with her hands,

"There was just

        this   and   this

and in between it was all commas."

44

Incident Four

Of course I didn't know that she was dying, when she was dying. I was alone. Everyone was asleep. I felt then that I needed all her books. Immediately. By my side.

I brought them into bed with me. We lay there warm and at ease together. I turned pages and read. I was suffused with pleasure. It was not excitement, but pleasure, keen contentment. This is how I felt that night. I feel asleep with a book open to the page that began "A Beautiful Voyage."

Perhaps the most unearthly of experiences is to feel so thoroughly at ease, so full with trust that, for once, the body is not a boundary that hems one in.

PHOTOGRAPH #5

Notice that this photograph is taken in the same room that was depicted in Photograph #4. However, the central focus of this photo is the bedding and the way a stack of books blends seamlessly with the curves of sheet, pillows, blanket.

The Nature of Association

That was a rare occasion however, not something that can be replicated, that quiet pleasure. More likely, more common for us humans is the life as indirection, the practice of ritual that would make indirection seem more linear and purposeful. An effective working out of associations.

For example, for a long time I have accorded to certain actions the recollection of absent people:

Putting lotion on after a shower makes me think of _____ .

The smell of Pear Soap brings to mind _____ .

The rough blue paper of a chapbook signifies _____ .

Most consistent of these instances: There is an enlarged pore on my upper left arm. Every time I look at it, I think of _____ . Every few weeks, I pinch at the edges of this pore until a thin line of exudate comes out. It is so fine that it looks like a tiny bit of white thread. I look at this, and then I press it between my fingers and it then disappears. All that's left is a mild smell of selfness. Whose?

Then I look at the empty pore, with its swollen edges, and this pleases and justifies me.

I hope you understand this and its relation to haunting. Embodiment always troubles us, but here you could have no clearer example of its effect.

PHOTOGRAPH #6

This is an otherwise unremarkable photograph of a woman's bare upper arm. Notice the perfectly circular pore about 4 inches from where the arm curves upward to the shoulder.

Incidents Five and Six

I have been frustrated in trying to sort out my reports of Incidents Five and Six. Both are so utterly typical that they resist depiction. The one event for its cliché quality and the other for its mundanity even though its context is not what is typically called a haunting. My decision has been to combine the two instances into a single account.

Let me say that the summer solstice is the longest day of the year.

Let me say that trauma lingers well past its ostensible duration.

That is what we are discussing here: duration.

We were out of the country and wandering through an ash grove. We passed through to a lake where we waded briefly and then moved back through the darkness of the grove to our accommodation in an old house where we went to sleep in nocturnal daylight.

We had been friends, I thought, true friends. But in this life, the idea of trueness is ridiculous. Is trueness proximity? Apparently it is not duration; haunting in this case is the lack of duration.

In the garden there were strawberries the size of a fist. A colossal tree that extended the girth and height of its hillside. We went into the great, empty house and fell asleep while it was still light outside, but nonetheless late.

Here is a ghost: an entity that stands by without comment while you are attacked, while you are subject to destruction. The ghost must always take care of itself.

When darkness has finally arrived, we are fully asleep. Click. I wake up to hear the door click. It was not volume but precision that attracted my ear.

"How would *you* know that?" asks the ghost.

Why does no one else wake up when this kind of thing happens? I get up and pull the door firmly closed, snapped shut.

This ghost is frustrated because I am not compliant. It extends an invitation, but it expects me to ignore that its hospitality is not sincere. The invitation is muddied by an insincere claim of forgetfulness.

The door opens again, precisely. Click.

If a ghost is marked by the quality of being incessant, can it also be characterized by its ability to forget, by its tendency to fail to recognize itself? Lack of self-recognition drives the ghost into a site that is not its own, the emptiness of an other. Peremptory, insistent. The site of the haunting may resist that occupying force, may object to the insult on its integrity. The site objects to the insult on its greater hospitality.

All night long the door clicks and opens. Shutting the door, checking the hallway and stairs, making sure no draft is sifting through the window and loosening the door in its jamb. Finally, I haul all our luggage to the doorway and prop it closed; I fall asleep to the door clicking uselessly, repeatedly, ajar in its frame.

"Well," says the ghost to its host, "I'll reject you if you continue to be of so little use to me." Its host responds by complaining of offenses to her person; the ghost had uttered insults that were clearly audible. The ghost scoffs dismissively: "I thought you didn't overhear me."

PHOTOGRAPH #7

This photograph is problematic, both because it is a double exposure and because the glare of late day (solstice) sunlight has somehow overexposed both images.

"It will cluster around your neck, your wrists, a God closer than our jugular. It's not personal. I am giving to your indistinction, what blends with the outside, cobbled into some passable ghost."

—Charity Stebbins

"the shape of what my voice

in my mouth is after the geography dies?"

"Swamped with the short ghosts of

breath"

—Julie Doxsee

Story

My favorite ghost story is called "The Beckoning Fair One."

A man moves into a house that has stood empty for a long time.

He hums a tune.

He is forever humming this tune. Out on the street, a trades-man overhears and remarks that it's been many years since that pretty melody was popular.

One day at home, the man realizes that the tap in the sink is drip-ping. He hears the same song he has been incessantly humming.

A faucet may advance, out of its emptiness, a melody.
Water may, of course, leak drops of itself from the conduit that dispenses water.

The story never makes a point that the man drank what issued from this tap.

We are left to speculate how the tune transported itself from an inactive faucet to the throat of the man.

PHOTOGRAPH #8

This is a commercial photograph of the book *Widdershins* by Oliver Onions, published by Dover Books. "The Beckoning Fair One" is one of the stories found in this collection.

ELIZABETH ROBINSON has published thirteen books of poetry; the most recent of these is *Counterpart*. A previous winner of the National Poetry Series, she is also the recipient of grants from the Fund for Poetry and the Foundation for Contemporary Arts. She coedits both Instance Press and the Etherdome Chapbook series, and she has taught at Naropa University; the University of Colorado, Boulder; the University of San Francisco; and the Iowa Writers' Workshop. Robinson is the 2012 and 2013 Hugo Fellow at the University of Montana.